Pebble
Plus

Media Literacy for Kids

Learning About
Fact and Opinion

by Martha E. H. Rustad

Consulting Editor: Gail Saunders-Smith, PhD

Consultant: JoAnne DeLurey Reed
Librarian and Teacher, Scroggins Elementary School
Houston, Texas

CAPSTONE PRESS
a capstone imprint

Pebble Plus is published by Capstone Press,
1710 Roe Crest Drive, North Mankato, Minnesota 56003
www.capstonepub.com

Library of Congress Cataloging-in-Publication Data
Rustad, Martha E. H. (Martha Elizabeth Hillman), 1975–
 Learning about fact and opinion / by Martha E. H. Rustad.
     pages cm.—(Pebble plus. Media literacy for kids)
 Includes bibliographical references and index.
   ISBN 978-1-4914-1831-4 (library binding)—ISBN 978-1-4914-1836-9 (ebook pdf)
1. Media literacy—Juvenile literature. 2. Journalism—Juvenile literature. 3. Mass
media—Objectivity—Juvenile literature. I. Title.

P96.M4R867 2015
302.23—dc23   2014023677

Editorial Credits
Erika L. Shores, editor; Sarah Bennett, designer; Gene Bentdahl, production specialist

Photo Credits
All photos Capstone Studio: Karon Dubke except: Alamy: Robert Fried, 15; Shutterstock:
grmarc, 21 (inset trumpet), Petr Jilek, cover, Pressmaster, 17 (inset), Rita Kochmarjova, 22,
RTimages, 17 (newspaper), Taisa, 17 (background)

Note to Parents and Teachers

The Media Literacy for Kids set supports Common Core State Standards
related to language arts. This book describes and illustrates facts and
opinions. The images support early readers in understanding the
text. The repetition of words and phrases helps early readers learn
new words. This book also introduces early readers to subject-specific
vocabulary words, which are defined in the Glossary section. Early
readers may need assistance to read some words and to use the Table of
Contents, Glossary, Read More, Internet Sites, Critical Thinking Using
the Common Core, and Index sections of the book.

Printed in the United States of America in North Mankato, Minnesota.
062015   009031R

Table of Contents

Telling Fact from Opinion

How do you know if something

is a fact or an opinion?

Learning the difference

between them is important.

Facts are true. We check facts

by finding evidence.

We ask a trusted source

for proof.

Fun Fact
The first day of winter is called the winter solstice.

Winter

Winter is the season between autumn and spring. In the Northern Hemisphere, the first day of winter is December 21 or 22. Winter lasts for three months. Winter is the coldest season of the year.

hemisphere
one half of Earth

Opinions tell feelings or ideas.

We can't prove opinions

are true. Opinions can start

with "I think," "I feel,"

or "I like."

"Snakes are reptiles."

This statement is a fact.

We can find proof.

Everyone agrees snakes

are reptiles.

"Snakes are the best pets!"

This is an opinion.

Not everyone thinks snakes

make good pets.

Check the Source

Knowing who created the

information helps you decide

if it is fact or opinion. Reporters

write news articles. A reporter's

job is to check facts in articles.

15

Editorials show writers or speakers sharing their opinions. They often use facts that support a belief. But facts that don't support the belief are left out.

OUR VIEW

Kids Should Go to School Year-Round

It is time to think about changing the way our students attend school. Research from a local university shows students at year-round schools learn more. Without a summer break, students won't forget what they have learned.

17

Anyone can write online wikis and blogs. People share ideas. They may say something is a fact when it is not. Readers must check other sources.

Edit Post

Title

All Video Games Are Bad for Kids

Permalink: http://connect.capstonepub.com/2014/08/title.html

Body

Formatting

Too many kids spend all their time in front of screens. Are video games getting in the way of ed
Yes!

Reader Beware!

Pay attention and think carefully.

Check sources. Decide if what

you see or hear is a fact

or an opinion.

Vote Ellen
for
Student Council

She's the best choice!

Join Band!

Everyone has fun!

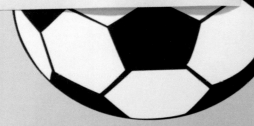
Soccer
Try-outs

April 15

Chess Club
meets today at 3!

Doggy Why's?
Copyright 2011 Northso
978-0-7358-4014-0

Activity: Discovering Facts and Opinions

Test a friend's knowledge about facts and opinions by doing this fun activity.

1. Look at this picture of a puppy and a kitten.

2. Using sticky notes, write facts about the photo. Remember a fact is something you can prove. Write as many statements of fact as you can.

3. What opinions do you have about the picture? Write as many opinions as you can about the picture. Remember opinions deal with feelings.

4. Now make two columns on the large sheet of paper. Label one "Facts" and label the other "Opinions."

5. Ask your friend to read all the statements you made about the photo.

What You Need

pad of sticky notes

pencil

marker

large sheet of paper

6. Have your friend decide which sticky notes belong in the "Facts" column and which ones belong in the "Opinions" column.

7. Try this activity again using a different photo. This time have your friend write the facts and opinions. Then you decide which are facts and which are opinions.

Glossary

blog—a personal website which includes the author's thoughts, opinions, and links

editorial—a written or spoken opinion about an important topic or problem

evidence—information, items, and facts that help prove something is true or false

online—to be connected to the Internet

proof—a way to show something is true

reporter—a person who researches and writes stories for news organizations

reptile—a cold-blooded animal with scales that lays eggs

source—a writer or speaker that gives information; books, newspapers, and other written information are also sources

wiki—a group website that tells the thoughts and opinions of many people

Read More

Gaines, Ann Graham. *Master the Library and Media Center.* Ace It! Information Literacy Series. Berkeley Heights, N.J.: Enslow Publishers, 2009.

McCurry, Kristen. *Pick a Picture, Write an Opinion!* Little Scribe. North Mankato, Minn.: Capstone Press, 2014.

Internet Sites

FactHound offers a safe, fun way to find Internet sites related to this book. All of the sites on FactHound have been researched by our staff.

Here's all you do:

Visit *www.facthound.com*

Type in this code: 9781491418314

 Check out projects, games and lots more at **www.capstonekids.com**

Critical Thinking Using the Common Core

What is an editorial? (Key Ideas and Details)

Look at page 21. Identify one poster that tells an opinion. Identify one poster that tells a fact. How did you know the difference? (Integration of Knowledge and Details)

Index

Word Count: 189
Grade: 1
Early-Intervention Level: 21